Finance Directors

D1638534

BDO Stoy Hayward specialises in helping businesses, whether start-ups or multinationals, to grow. By working directly with fast-track organisations and the entrepreneurs behind them, we've developed a robust understanding of the factors that govern business growth. BDO Stoy Hayward is a member of the BDO International network, the world's fifth largest accountancy organisation, with representation in more than ninety countries.

Rupert Merson is a partner in BDO Stoy Hayward, where he specialises in helping growing businesses with their people and organisational development problems. Rupert took first-class honours and a university prize in English from Oxford University. He is a chartered accountant and a Fellow of the Chartered Institute of Personnel and Development. He teaches a course on the management of the growing business at London Business School and writes frequently in the national press. He lives in south London with his wife and four children. He's a musician on the side.

Finance Directors

A BDO Stoy Hayward Guide for
Growing Businesses

Rupert Merson

P

PROFILE BOOKS

First published in Great Britain in 2003 by
PROFILE BOOKS LTD
58A Hatton Garden
London EC1N 8LX
www.profilebooks.co.uk

A CIP catalogue record for this book is available from the British Library.

ISBN 1 86197 454 X

Typeset in Galliard by MacGuru Ltd
info@macguru.org.uk

Printed in Great Britain by
Bookmarque, Croydon, Surrey

While care has been taken to ensure the accuracy of the contents of this book,
it is intended to provide general guidance only and does not constitute
professional advice.

Contents

The governor of all that exists …

THIS BOOK IS ABOUT the role of the finance director in businesses with ambitions to grow.

These businesses tend to be young and entrepreneurial. They also tend to be owned by the people who manage them – quite often the individual or individuals who founded them.

On the other hand, a growing business's finance director is unlikely to have been in from the beginning. Accountants are famously not entrepreneurial, and some would argue that

> **'When you were twenty-one,** you decided to become an accountant. That's about the least entrepreneurial thing any human being could choose to do …'

the last thing you want in an accountant is the sort of qualities you might praise in an entrepreneur. But a growing business will not grow far or fast without a decent finance director. And there is surprisingly little in print about the peculiar experience of working as a finance director in an entrepreneurial business.

In describing the role of the finance director attention often turns to the relationship between the finance director

'The relationship between the founder and the new finance director is necessarily not always an easy one.'

and the people who put the business together in the first place. The Head of the Treasury of Upper Egypt during the Old Kingdom took for himself the title of 'Governor of all that exists and all that does not exist.'[1] Many entrepreneurs and business owners, thinking nostalgically of the days before they had a finance director, will probably argue that things haven't changed much since 2500 BC. The relationship between the founder and her new finance director is necessarily not always an easy one. In a young business the role of the finance management is about much more than finance – it's about people even more than profit. The role of the finance director in a growing business in particular is about the functioning of the top management team, and the distribution of power.

Many management writers[2] when looking at directors have drawn a distinction between creative, inspirational, enthusiastic types, and organised, disciplined, sensible managerial types, using the labels 'leader' for the former and 'manager' for the latter. But the distinction has also been usefully applied to entrepreneurs and other members of the management team.

Most businesses start high on leadership and low on management.[3] If they are to stand a chance of developing into something that is remotely sustainable, then they will need more of those qualities of energy, inspiration and creativity. There is little to 'manage' that can't be done simply by force of personality. A business in its early stages will thus move from 1 to 2 if it is to evolve – dominated by individuals with qualities of 'leadership'.

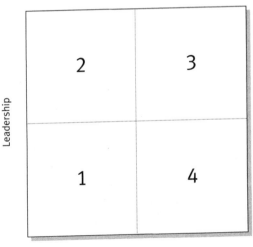

But things change. As Jeremy Newman of BDO Stoy Hayward writes:

New businesses are started by entrepreneurs who, through some combination of wisdom and luck, create and implement a successful business strategy. The business expands and profits grow and with this comes the need to hire professional managers. So people are recruited and promoted to manage, to cope with the growing bureaucracy and to prevent things getting out of control. And so the organisation grows and management grows to cope with it.[4]

The introduction of 'management' heralds reporting timetables, appraisal schemes, formal agendas and other manifestations of the way to run a 'proper' business. From an

> **'There are only three types of problems** in growing businesses: owner problems, manager problems, and owner-manager problems.'

organisation that thrives on the petrol vapour of entrepreneurship and the rushing around after the next sale, the new business inevitably evolves into one in which disciplined forces of management have far more influence. The business moves from 2 to 3. Of course, 3, where leadership and management styles hold each other in balance, is the ideal position for the senior team to reach. ('Top right' is usually the place to be in all of these two-by-two boxes.) You want enough business discipline to sustain the business, but not too much so that the qualities of entrepreneurship and leadership are damaged.

For many businesses, however, staying 'top right' sounds good in theory, but is difficult to achieve in practice. Some entrepreneurs ('leaders') feel they are obliged to turn into managers, or at least develop management capability. But although human beings can change and develop, rare indeed is the individual who can operate comfortably at both ends of the leadership/management spectrum. Other entrepreneurs,

> **'As our company grows,** the essence that binds us together will be hard to maintain.'

however, might seek to ensure that management expertise is recruited and thus provided by others (including the FD, of course) – allowing the entrepreneur the illusion of thinking that his role doesn't need to change that much. Unfortunately, managers and leaders have a tendency not to see to eye to eye, and an unchanging entrepreneur is on target for an almighty conflict with a new management team – which often results in the departure of one or the other, before or after damage to the business. Indeed, a reluctance to face up to the consequences of the tension leads some businesses to duck the problem in the first place. But businesses have no choice other than to introduce management infrastructure if they are serious about sustainable growth. Family businesses in particular, where blood is often thicker than mineral water, are particularly prone to deferring the necessary professionalisation of management.

And it is true that once in, the management force can do damage as well as good. The tendency for many with a managerial bent is to assume that the management force is more important than the entrepreneurial one – indeed this is the natural tendency of much Western business thinking. As Jeremy Newman writes: 'This in turn stifles leadership and

> **'In one new consultancy business** I was FD in, the MD came back from a management course, filled with the desire to implement detailed controls and procedures. I discussed these with him and drafted the required policies. We explained these to the rest of the management team and the MD was very vocal in his belief that he wanted to implement 'big company structures' in his growing business. At the end of the first month, I highlighted several instances where these new procedures had not been followed, and expenses had been incurred without authorisation. The main culprit was the MD. His reaction was one of horror – in all our discussions, he had never imagined that he would be expected to follow these procedures. He saw himself as being above this level.'

encourages management. Because the business is successful, managers begin to believe that they are the best, and their idiosyncrasies become part of the culture of the organisation.'

But whereas it is certainly true that a business without decent management will not survive for long, a business in which the management impulse takes over and squeezes the entrepreneurial spirit out of the organisation will turn into yet another over-managed, under-inspired, middle-aged business on a glide-path to history. Premature ageing in an organisation is almost as worrying as a refusal to let the organisation grow up. Such premature ageing is particularly a feature of 'start-ups' established by major blue chips, making the mistaken assumption that a small business is just a small version of a big one. I was once introduced to just such a start-up, founded as a stand-alone joint venture by two major PLCs. The new MD was keen to talk about 'establishing an entrepreneurial culture', but in the same meeting

> **'I founded a business** because I was fed up with the bureaucracy of the firm I worked in. And then one day I was horrified to find I had created just the sort of business I had wanted to escape from in the first place ...'

was anxious to discuss implementing a defined benefit pension scheme – a sure sign of a business on its way to being old before its time. And there are lots of businesses like this – and lots of finance directors who have been blamed for having set them on that path. In this context, isn't it interesting how many finance directors succeed the entrepreneur as chief executive in young businesses? Entrepreneurs and finance directors both need to be wary of delusions of grandeur as the business grows. They each bring different things to the growing business, and each needs to be wary of believing he can do the job of the other.

As well as illustrating a useful contrast between the entrepreneur and the finance director, the leadership vs. management model outlines what is for many young businesses a key feature of the history of their growth and development. All businesses have to pass through stages in their evolution, and the managerial, organisational, strategic and operational imperatives differ significantly from one stage to the next. In short, as well as growing, businesses have to grow up. Growth is thus all about change. Although all businesses change, change in small, fast-growing businesses is more extreme and faster than in large businesses – indeed the

'Rare indeed is the individual who can operate comfortably at both ends of the leadership/management spectrum.'

fastest-growing businesses need to be delivering organisational change almost before it is needed.

In recent years this view of organisational evolution has been questioned. In particular, some commentators have argued that the dot.coms illustrated that it was possible to emerge from the womb fully formed, without having passed through the formative early stages and the transformations worked in those stages. However, the subsequent failure of many of the same dot.coms has led to a return to basic business thinking about growth. As with small children, those early years can be uncomfortable – but you risk a lot if you try to become an adult without them.

This book is aimed at both the entrepreneur minded to add a finance director to his team, and at the would-be finance director in an entrepreneurial business with ambitions to grow. It addresses the role of the key individuals behind a business as it wrestles with the challenges and changes presented by growth. These challenges are very different from those faced by managers in big businesses. A small business is not a small big business – such a mindset is patronising and runs the risk of underestimating the real problems confronting young and growing businesses. In Amar Bhide's words, 'The organisational weaknesses and imperfections that entrepreneurs confront every day would cause the managers of a mature company to panic.'[5] Recognising that most finance directors are likely to be over-educated in the problems of big business, and under-educated in the problems of smaller businesses, this book is offered as a comfort in those moments when those waves of panic might seem to be coming on.

- Businesses have to grow up as well as grow. A finance director is a symptom of the change as well as a driving force behind it
- Many businesses suffer from the temptation to over-manage and under-lead
- Growth is all about change
- Small businesses are not small big businesses

2

The finance director – why and when and who and how much

Why and when?

The decision to add to the senior management team is amongst the most critical of all decisions for the young business. Who you recruit and why will have a crucial impact on the future direction of the business. The target is to have a business that is set up to run itself with the appropriate checks, balances and warning lights; a business that is managed by the collective effort of a team rather than by sheer force of personality. A business dominated by personality will never be sustainable. What will happen to it when the

> **'You never know** you need a finance director until you don't have one.'

personality steps away? Many entrepreneurs therefore find that as the business matures further growth is as much about giving up control as about putting controls in. Giving control away is all to do with being mature about delegation and management. But what is delegated and to whom will have a significant influence on the direction of the business.

Some will recruit sales and marketing expertise in a conviction that building the top line is the most significant challenge. Too few business founders, on the other hand, look to the finance director as the key first recruit to the top team. Too many growing businesses leave the financial levers of their business either in the hands of someone without sufficient capability or in the hands of no one at all until far too late. In part this is the mistaken consequence of an instinctive determination to preserve the entrepreneurial spirit in the young business. For many entrepreneurs, an accountant will add to cost but not to profit, and spending lots on defence is counter-intuitive if your natural inclination is to attack. The right time for the first finance director is of course impossible to define, but is sooner rather than later.

To be fair, businesses look to recruit a finance director earlier now than they did in the past. One sizeable retail chain reached a listing on the Stock Exchange without a finance director. Even when it set about recruiting someone to handle 'legal issues', what the board were really worried about was finding someone to handle retail/liquor licences and so on. Financial regulation was not on their agenda. This role ultimately turned into company secretary – and only then by way of a slow process of evolution into someone who called himself the finance director. Of course the individual had the title – but he didn't have the skills. It was only the experience of the listing that caused the chain to recruit a finance director worthy of the title.

All this was twenty years ago – businesses are unlikely to get this far without a good finance director nowadays. For some years running a business of any size has required delicate footsteps through minefields of increasing legal and regulatory complexity. A business without someone who knows the way through the minefield is looking for disaster. And the pace of business has quickened enormously over the last twenty years, putting pressure on internal measurement and management systems. In a post-Enron, post-Worldcom world, the credibility of a business with ambition but

> '**"I cut my own sandwiches** and I keep my own books" defines for many the key difference between the "entrepreneur" and the "chief executive".'

without good financial direction will be questioned even more. A business that wants to be taken seriously by investors must have an effective finance director influencing business strategy and exerting management control.

Businesses with ambition see the balance brought to a team by a finance director as a huge benefit. It's back to the balance between leadership and management. 'Without me, the business wouldn't be there,' writes Julian Metcalfe of his take-away sandwich business, Pret a Manger. 'And without him, it wouldn't work,' he writes of his founding-partner, Sinclair Beecham.[6] Recognising and capitalising on the different contributions that people bring to the growing business and successfully building a team out of them will dramatically increase the chances of growth. A good finance director and an effective entrepreneur working in tandem can be an exceptionally powerful team.

Who?

Part of the problem of recruiting the first finance director

'Career development is exceptionally difficult for accounts staff within a growing business – there isn't the scale necessary to provide a career path for the capable individual.'

worthy of the title is recognising that someone in the business – if not the founder herself – is likely to have pretensions to the role, even if not the title already. Before you recruit your first finance director you have to find (and sometimes fire) the current one. Too often the book-keeper is called finance director, but not given the pay rise or the equity – always a good sign that they are FD in title but not role. Good FDs cost money.

There are good reasons why junior accounting staff in a growing business are unlikely to 'grow with the business' into the role of finance director. Career development is exceptionally difficult for accounts staff within a growing business – there isn't the scale necessary to provide a career path for the capable individual. As a finance director of

> **'I've come across a situation** where the FD was obsessed with daily reports and haranguing sales people about minutiae. He generated a boxful of reports every day and would spend most of the day going through them with a red pen. Meanwhile, in the office beside him, huge commercial decisions were being made in his absence. His lack of knowledge about what was going on in the business almost brought the business to its knees because nobody was looking at the cashflow impact of certain key decisions.'

several growing businesses puts it: 'Even if you are lucky enough to find a financial controller with director potential, you're highly unlikely to keep her for long.' The likelihood is therefore that the first finance director – and the second, and the third – in a growing business will come from outside.

What sort of individual should the growing business be looking for? You want someone who knows how sizeable businesses are run, because that is what you are trying to build. But at the same time you need them to be in sympathy with the demands of running a smaller business, because that is what you've got. You need them to be excited by change, because in moving from small to big that is exactly what they go through. One entrepreneur I know observes that when interviewing potential business managers he asks candidates what they think their most important task will be. The answer he is looking for is something about the need to recruit their own successors. Someone too used to big business will see this as a threat: someone who understands instinctively the growing business will see this as what growth is all about. As the successful manager grows with the business into a bigger job, so someone will be needed to take the smaller one.

The business needs more than simply an accountant, if by accountant we understand someone who is just good at ensuring that all the information is collated, that none leaks out, and that it is reported in the correct way. The growing

> '**On my first day as FD** at a prestigious London hotel, the general manager remarked, "I can't understand why we have such trouble retaining our junior accounts staff." When I was brought to the accounts office, I understood why – the staff were "housed" in a dark room, infested with mice, and had to wear dust masks all day because of extensive building works taking place outside.'

business needs someone who will influence the strategy and management of the business. This implies someone who can stand up to the founders, tell the story told by the figures with conviction, and provide an intellectual and commercial rigour to corporate decision-taking. Growing businesses don't need accountants so much as risk-managers. As one finance director says, 'Intellectual rigour – being able to think clearly about the business – is the most important character-istic of an FD.' The relationship between the finance director and the rest of the team is critical, and a separate chapter is devoted to it later.

It is *possible* to imagine a finance director without a pro-fessional accounting qualification, but only just. The role requires technical know-how in accounting and tax, systems and controls, financial and human resource management, law and regulation. At the very least a finance director should add 'significantly to the technical capability of the senior team. If this is delegation, therefore, it is 'added-value delegation'. If the new finance director is not better than the team, she won't change it. A qualified chartered or certified accountant

> **'Owner-managers think** they know everything about their business. At one retail chain, the owners confidently told me that the shop margin should be 21 per cent. I looked at the management accounts for the current year and the margin was 17 per cent. When I questioned this difference they said that there was a lot of theft and fraud, and told me about all the complex systems they had just put in place to combat this. Despite all this effort and expense, the following month's margin was also 17 per cent. I then analysed the theoretical margin and found that it should only be 17 per cent. Over time, the margin had been eroded by a different product mix, but the owners had never realised this. The owner-manager can often quote figures with such authority that it can be difficult for a new FD to question her.'

is more likely to have the know-how than most, and the certificate helps reinforce credibility. MBAs have made it to the role of finance director in big business. But the accounting department of a big business will be stuffed with accounting qualifications even if the FD doesn't have any. In a younger growing business, an unqualified finance director will be much more exposed.

In the UK qualified accountants come with all sorts of experience. Chartered accountants mostly start out 'in the profession'. Businesses looking for their first finance director often find candidates looking for their first finance director-ships. Individuals who come straight from qualifying would be unlikely to have the breadth of experience necessary. On the other hand, a candidate at partner level moving to a new role away from the profession may find it difficult to adjust to life on the outside. As one finance director said, 'You're very closeted in the profession, surrounded by like-minded people with similar outlooks and similar backgrounds.' The best finance director for the growing business is someone who has spent some time 'doing something different', argues one of the senior partners at BDO Stoy Hayward. A leading venture capitalist agrees – he will only invest in businesses with 'quality finance directors' – but he prefers his finance directors to have had some experience outside finance alto-gether. Some accountants qualifying from big accounting firms have only seen the inside of big businesses – and that just isn't enough for a senior office holder in a younger, growing business.

There are other routes than the chartered to qualifying as an accountant, however – though the fact that all the recog-nised institutes like to call themselves 'chartered' hardly makes for clarity. Chartered management accountants will almost definitely have earned their experience inside account-ing departments rather than accounting firms. On the one hand this might seem a plus – at least they will have trained in the real world. This is true, but on the other hand, younger growing businesses do not often take on trainees. Such accountants may have experience only of big businesses – and only of one or two. Further, their experience of inter-nal, management accounting may be first class, but their exposure to statutory accounting, tax and the rest may be

'The first finance director in the growing business need not be full-time. Part-time qualified accountants are in increasing supply – not least owing to the significant increase in women in the profession.'

slender. Chartered certified accountants sit somewhere between management accountants and chartered accountants. They may have experience of public practice, or not. In summary, you need a qualified accountant for sure – but you need to read the small print, and test it as well.

The first finance director in the growing business need not be full-time. Part-time qualified accountants are in increasing supply – not least owing to the significant increase in women in the profession, many of whom want roles that offer opportunity plus greater flexibility for spending time at home. And there are also organisations that specialise in providing financial management services to businesses not big enough to require full-time help.

Given that the decision to add to the top team is probably the most important that any business founder will take, too

> **'An entrepreneur needs** to recruit someone with fundamentally different skills and outlook from himself – and the temptation to be impressed in interview with people who agree with you is enormous ...'

much attention is paid to 'gut feel' rather than rational analysis in recruitment and selection processes. Too many founders are too impressed by candidates in their own image, or – even worse – candidates who are good at saying 'yes', but will not provide the robust challenge needed within the top team of any business. An entrepreneur looking for a finance director will have to give serious thought to what she wants and what the finance director will be doing, and then she will have to invest serious time in ensuring her selection processes and interviews root out what she needs to know. The discipline of drawing up a 'job specification' and a 'role specification' doesn't need expertise, and will dramatically improve the chances of recruiting the right individual. Serious attention needs to be paid to how the role is 'sold' to the candidate. When you're selling your own business to a candidate the temptation to paint a picture without the warts is dangerous. When growing a business you need people with experience of where you are going – the next stage of evolution. But the new member of the team also needs to be under no illusions as to the reality of the business as it is now. And in a growing business things can change so quickly that the job will have changed before the new recruit has even served her notice period with her old employer.

How much?

Finding the right candidate is a serious challenge – working out how to pay her can be even worse. A worthwhile finance director is expensive in the sense that she might be your highest-paid employee – but as one venture capitalist's view puts it: 'I always tell companies we're looking to invest in that a quality finance director will more than pay for herself

> **'The finance director is usually** under-rewarded compared to the CEO (who is usually over-rewarded!).' *Venture Capitalist*

within a year.' And one successful entrepreneur observes that 'A good finance director is a business angel who brings something worth much more than money.' But many businesses without a decent finance director will still argue they can't afford one.

Unsurprisingly, many entrepreneurs look for ways of structuring a package that allows the business to keep the cake whilst giving the candidate the illusion of enjoying eating it. Performance-related remuneration is relevant in this context. An HR director in a major professional services firm once told me that a bonus was an excuse not to pay someone properly in the first place. There is some truth in this – linking pay to performance is often used by smaller businesses as a mechanism for ensuring that expensive staff pay for themselves, and there is hardly anything wrong with that.

Unfortunately, the mechanics of connecting pay to performance are difficult to establish effectively. If you want individuals to be *influenced* by their remuneration then you should avoid making the package too complicated. Build in too many variables, and most human beings will throw their hands in the air and carry on doing what they would have done had they not been given performance-related pay in the first place. Then the only people to benefit from the scheme will be the consultants paid for setting it up. On the other hand, the reality is that most of the senior team members' roles *are* complicated, and those that occupy them are responsible for dozens of variables. To connect remuneration to just a selection is to invite dysfunctional behaviour as staff are encouraged to focus on those aspects of their roles which will increase their income at the expense of those that do not. For a role like finance director in a private business, it can be difficult coming up with performance targets that are personal. Indeed, it is often best to worry not so much about the individual as about corporate performance when determining bonuses and other forms of remuneration. If the business does well, then the individual will do well. But of course, though this might address affordability it doesn't necessarily provide a motivating incentive for the finance director herself. Her efforts might be indispensable, but the finance director can't deliver a successful business on her own.

The tidiest way of connecting a finance director's remuneration to the performance of the business is to give him

'Staff are encouraged to focus on those aspects of their roles which will increase their income at the expense of those that do not. For a role like finance director in a private business, it can be difficult.'

shares. Certainly this can be a good step towards aligning the interests of the director with the interests of the business. It is also a mechanism for fostering alignment between the entrepreneur and the finance director. Using equity as an incentive should not be confused with using cash. Cash is inherently short-term. Equity rewards the long term. 'Equity should be used to foster or reward commitment,' argues entrepreneur, venture capitalist and London Business School Fellow John Bates. If you want to recruit or reward

'The finance director should be passionate enough about the business to at least want equity in it.' *Private equity investor*

knowledge, or experience, you should be prepared to pay for it when you use it – with cash. Many businesses are not this discriminating. Equity or quasi-equity is now an expected component of the package of a senior member of any business, big or small, public or private, and it's often forgotten that it used to be rare for the finance director or indeed any other director to get equity at all. To a certain extent finance directors get equity because that's what happens.

Giving and receiving shares can be troublesome. Being given a slice of the equity of an unlisted company is not the same as being given equity in a business whose shares have a ready market. To be given equity inevitably begs questions about when those shares might be sold and in what circumstances. A new member of the management team with equity is thus likely to have at the very least half an eye on a financial strategy that will enable him to realise his investment. We'll discuss this more later, but many finance directors are surprised to find how common it is for entrepreneurs not to have given serious thought to 'exit'. At the very least therefore a discussion about equity or equity-based remuneration will force a discussion about the alignment of personal and corporate objectives.

On the other hand, from the founder-shareholders' perspective, the prospect of giving away equity can look like giving away something for nothing. But if the new team member is the difference that will make your business grow, then you should remember that a smaller share of a well-managed larger business can be worth much more than the whole of a less-well-managed smaller business. A common mistake is to confuse ownership with control. You can afford to share major slugs of equity with others without losing control of the business. Many never appreciate the importance of this distinction, nor the flexibility it offers.

For many businesses thinking about equity as incentive, share options can look like another way of having your cake and eating it at the same time. Assuming options are granted at least at current business value, an option will only become a share if the business increases in value. It's easy to be cynical about options. Dot.coms in the last few years have shed share options like confetti – which has not improved their street credibility. Option schemes are inherently complicated and expensive to establish. And because the individual probably won't have to give anything for them at the outset it's easy to see them as all gain and no pain – and therefore not nearly so great a motivation as might at first appear. Additionally, as with equity, options are only meaningful if the

---

- Recruit a proper finance director sooner rather than later
- The finance director has to wrestle with the business – not just the finance
- Recruit a qualified accountant with experience of the younger business – and preferably general commercial experience as well
- Giving a finance director equity is a good way of aligning personal and corporate interests. But it isn't as simple as that …
- Introducing the first new members to a senior management team is among the most critical acts a business will ever perform. Give it the attention it deserves before, during and after the recruitment exercise
- Structuring the appropriate remuneration package is essential
- A good finance director is expensive – but she will pay for herself within a reasonable timeframe

---

holder can at least imagine a time when they are realisable. On the other hand, even if you don't think they're a good idea, the Chancellor does, and there are some exceptionally tax-efficient options mechanisms around, particularly for the smaller, private business. Remember, however, not to let tax complicate the picture. Tax is the cart, not the horse. Work out what you want to achieve, then work out the most tax-effective way of delivering it.

3

The finance director – and the rest of the management team

THE MOST IMPORTANT CHALLENGE when defining the role for any finance director in a young, entrepreneurial business is to define how the role relates to other members of the management team.

Joining the management team

Joining a team that has been running for a time and is thus already established is different from being there from the beginning. As far as the founding team is concerned, 'team' is perhaps too scientific a term for what is usually little more

> **'A friendship based on business** is more likely to last than a business based on friendship.' *John D Rockefeller, quoting his business partner*

than a group of friends. If the team starts with a proper finance director in place from the beginning there's a chance that things will be set up on a professional footing. A new finance director coming into an established team will often find that the professional relations between team members

'"Team" is perhaps too scientific a term for what is usually little more than a group of friends.'

have not been set up in a way that gives them the best chance of surviving a failure in the friendship – often the unfortunate consequence of even a successful business venture between friends. Four friends with 25 per cent each of the equity, for example, might start out with great intentions, but organisational stalemate could follow, for example if the four fall out and old friends then start taking sides and voting accordingly, locking decision-taking on key issues requiring shareholder approval. Founding partners need to ensure that the relationship between them is as well thought-through, structured and documented as that with a third party – and a finance director has a key role to play in this thinking and structuring. A CEO came to see me once wanting to sack his co-director, but worried by the cost of termination. Some years earlier when the business was established, both directors had written themselves service contracts containing two-year notice clauses. 'We did this to protect our positions against our "sleeping partner" who was non-executive, but who had provided the finance,' he said. 'We needed his help with the finance, but were worried what would happen if he turned against us.' The two executive directors were also, of course, entitled to use the notice clauses as defences against each other – something that had occurred to neither when the clauses were written. Having this sort of discussion when a business is founded is difficult and can appear like making funeral arrangements at a baptism. But difficult conversations early on may well mean the survival of the business later.

Joining an established team is a different and difficult experience for any finance director. Breaking into the senior team behind an *owner-managed* business brings its special challenges. For a start, the finance director's motivation is likely to be very different from that of the founders. The finance director will not have experienced the drama of

> **'It can also be a problem** if the MD and the FD work too closely together. In one of my FD roles the MD and I got on particularly well. We tended to speak to each other, make quick decisions and implement them. The management team meetings turned into information sessions – the MD would tell the rest of the team what we (the MD and the FD) had decided since the last meeting. This created a series of problems and we almost lost two key members of the team before we understood the error of our ways.'

founding something from nothing. The founders too have to recognise this – and resist the temptation of perpetually holding against the finance director the fact that he wasn't there from the start.

A finance director who joins the team after the start is thus both part of the team and apart from it, working with the others but also for them and supervising them. A key feature of the role is the way it sits on top of a Gordian knot of conflicting interests. In small, private companies the pressures of conflict can be more painful as the business will quite probably have no internal regulation or guidance for avoiding conflict or dealing with it when it arises. The relative inexperience of the directors only exacerbates the problem – and foists more responsibility on to the shoulders of the new finance director.

Owner-managers will struggle to sort out the conflict between their roles as *directors* and *shareholders*. The directors are charged with the governance and management of the company. Their job is to act in the interests of the company, not in their own. But when it comes to their role as shareholders it is much more a case of every man for himself. A shareholder is allowed to act in his own interests rather in the notional interests of the company of which he has chosen to be a member. The shareholders do not have a role running the business day to day, but pass this responsibility to the directors. What then of the director who owns shares? As a shareholder, a director attending a shareholders' meeting can in general vote in his own interests and not those of the company (though not in a board meeting). However, if he is a majority shareholder he is not allowed to discriminate against minority shareholders: if he does, the latter can object that the relevant resolutions are not in the interests of the company as a whole. A key occasion when conflict might raise its head is when one or more of the directors seek to effect a management buy-out. Of course, the decision to recommend approval of the MBO should be taken only by those board members not participating in the deal. However, it should always be remembered that it is *all* directors who have a responsibility for ensuring any transaction is in the best interests of the shareholders – including those fronting the deal itself. A director who is also a shareholder needs therefore to remember which hat he is wearing. He also needs to remember when he is wearing it – in a shareholders' meeting or a board meeting of the directors.

Owner-managers will struggle with more general conflicts between their own interests and their responsibilities as directors. Any director has to be careful to distinguish between his actions on behalf of the company and his actions in a personal capacity. As a director, an individual represents his company when he negotiates with others on his company's behalf. When signing documents, the director should make sure he discloses that he signs as a director of a company whose full name is given, otherwise he might be deemed to be signing as himself, and therefore be personally liable for the contracts. Conflicts between personal self-interest and the duty owed by a director to the company happen in the life-cycle of the growing business. Particular attention should be paid if the business is courting insolvency – when the interests of other stakeholders including employees and creditors also become influential. This is an important area and is covered in more detail at the end of this book.

The finance director is best positioned to manage and police these conflicts. Indeed, outsiders will look on him to do so. 'I hate the finance director who thinks his role is to act in the interests of the entrepreneur rather than the other stakeholders,' says one seasoned investor in smaller businesses. 'The good finance director will go in and find what's wrong and put it right,' says another – hinting at plenty of opportunity for conflict with other members of the team. Of course, conflict with the investor is also a real possibility. We discuss this key relationship more in Chapter 4.

Who's boss?

It's not uncommon to meet senior management teams in smaller businesses who claim to be teams of equals. I never believe it. A self-styled team of equals is usually one in which the boss is so much in charge that other members of the team daren't even challenge him on his claim that 'we're a team of equals'. The reality is that someone will always have to be in charge. She might not have the title of CEO or MD but in effect that is what she will be. Indeed in younger businesses titles can be misleading. I've dealt with small businesses that had two, even three 'managing directors'. I've also dealt with businesses with an MD, but where it was the FD who really called the shots. Second-generation family businesses often provide illustrations of 'joint managing directors', usually arising out of the reluctance of the first generation to choose between their children. It's rarely the first generation that has to pay the price for such indecisiveness.

Striking up the right relationship with the boss is critical – and many finance directors in growing businesses get off to the wrong start because they fail to understand the nature of the beast they are dealing with. Entrepreneurs are increasingly well researched but the knowledge gained has yet to filter into common business thinking.

Those who know nothing about entrepreneurs other than what they read in the Sunday supplements often assume that entrepreneurs are born, not bred – that they started when they were fourteen selling sweets at school and are all creative types who are also incorrigible extroverts – risk-junkies, desperate to make a quick million. Those in the know recognise that such people are the exception rather than the rule.

'Many finance directors in growing businesses get off to the wrong start because they fail to understand the nature of the beast they are dealing with.'

Understanding where entrepreneurs stand on money as a motivator is key for a finance director. The quick million is not necessarily their motivation (which is just as well ...). Two American academics argued in an article in May 2000 that there are essentially two types of entrepreneur. The 'primary goal' of one group is 'to prepare for a cash-out ... Maximising market value before the cash-out is their sole and abiding purpose.' On the other hand there are other

entrepreneurs driven by the aim of 'building an institution'.
Such individuals have essentially different aims:

> Accumulating wealth is important, but it is secondary to
> creating a company that is based on a deeply held set of
> values and that has a strong culture. These entrepreneurs
> are likely to subscribe to an egalitarian style that invites
> everyone's participation. They look to attract others who
> share their passion about the cause ... Their goal is to
> make a difference, not just to make money.[7]

For those interested in building a business, money is, of
course, important, particularly as a measure of success, but it
is a means not an end. Making money as a motivator is a
short-term mindset. Arguably many erstwhile leaders of tar-
nished dot.coms fell into this category. Some of these would-
be paper millionaires were often not nearly as interested in
the business venture itself as they were in the thought that
they might be able to create and sell off an enterprise in a
short time. This line of thinking has much more to do with
financial engineering or riding the wave in a boom economy
than it has to do with business creation. Building a business
has to be done with the long term in mind – and it is this sort
of activity that distinguishes entrepreneurship from financial
investment. Understanding this difference in motivation can
make all the difference for the finance director. In many
instances the finance director can help the entrepreneur
understand his own motivation.

Another important characteristic of entrepreneurs is the
spirit of independence, the wish to do their own thing in
their own way. To want to do something one way is often a
reaction against having seen it done the 'wrong' way. There is
something in entrepreneurship therefore that is essentially
reactive, and certainly something that requires a certain

amount of experience before taking root – even if it is experience of how not to do things. Perhaps it is unsurprising, therefore, that academic research often shows the average first-time entrepreneur to be reasonably well educated, to have had some good work experience, and to be in his or her thirties.[8] Finance directors working with entrepreneurs are often surprised by the hard business experience they have on their CVs – they underestimate it at their peril.

There is a key distinction between being an inventor and being an entrepreneur: the latter is a pragmatic role rather than a creative one – the difference is between what goes on inside the garden shed, and the effort required to get an idea out of the shed. Indeed, many entrepreneurs work best with other people's ideas rather than their own. Entrepreneurs, argues one Harvard professor, W. A. Sahlman, are people who make maximum use of intangible rather than tangible assets, not least because these are the only assets they are likely to have. Entrepreneurship is very much a 'can do and will do' state of mind despite the lack of resources: 'I don't have the building or the equipment, and I don't have the money or the people either. But I'm still going to do it.' At the heart of entrepreneurship therefore is a paradox: on the one hand it is all about making the abstract concrete; on the other hand it is all about not losing heart when the only thing you have on your side is the abstract. In these circumstances personality is often much more important than abilities or qualifications. An entrepreneur needs to have strong personal motivation to force the business into life, and in the early years it is important that the individual's personal motivation and goals are aligned with the corporate objectives of the business. As the business expands and particularly as expertise is added to the top team, the aspirations of the entrepreneur can increasingly be at odds with corporate objectives and corporate needs.

It is important for the finance director to understand an entrepreneur's attitude to risk. Research shows that entrepreneurs are more likely to see themselves as calculated risk takers than gamblers. This may come as a surprise to the public – and also to the average finance director. And the

> **'Friction can be useful** ... And don't expect it to come from your advisers ... It's left to the finance director to do the standing up and disagreeing ...'

public surely has a point: is it not self-evident that the entrepreneurial attitude to risk is somehow different from that of the normal human being or the career-employee, no matter how successful and ambitious? Maybe entrepreneurs just don't know how risk-friendly they are. Experimental evidence suggests that, statistically, individuals are more likely to take a risk to avoid a loss than to realise a gain.[9] Perhaps there is something in the entrepreneurial make-up that reverses this typical attitude to risk. It is not that an entrepreneurial venture is necessarily inherently more risky – rather it is that many an entrepreneur evaluates the risk differently. If this hypothesis is right it points to a marked contrast in the approach to risk between someone with an entrepreneurial mindset and – for example – someone with an accountancy background who might well be coming to a young business as finance director, for example. 'You've got to be a bit of a gambler,' says Julian Metcalfe of Pret a Manger. 'My partner's way of assessing a risk is to work out if we can afford to lose

'You should start as you mean to go on. One finance director remembers an early argument with a founder.'

the money. Mine is to do it anyway, because if you feel passionately about something it's probably going to work.'[10]

Getting it right from the beginning

You should start as you mean to go on. One finance director remembers an early argument with a founder. The founder was short of cash for a forthcoming holiday and so took a bit out of the business and thought nothing of it. No doubt he was surprised to find his finance director up in arms when he returned from the beach. 'You earn credibility on the small things, not the big ones,' the FD says, 'and it's credibility the

> **'Where an FD sits** can be really important. At an interview, the MD will go on about how he wants the FD to be his right hand, to be totally involved in all aspects of the business etc. I always ask where my desk or office is to be located. If I find that it is miles away from the MD, somewhere in the basement, I question whether the MD really wants an FD to be as he describes. Wouldn't you prefer your right hand to be close to you?'

new finance director needs most of all.' Another adds, 'The finance director provides the board with its most level-headed person.' The finance director might well need help in standing up to the founder, and a good non-executive can provide the best source of this assistance. In their very early days the finance director and a good non-executive are each other's best allies. Thereafter, of course, they need to become checks and balances on each other. This may all sound like wheeler-dealing and negotiation. Indeed, one FD sees being a good negotiator as a key skill in a finance director, with the other parties to the negotiations usually being the other members of the board.

Useful first steps for the growing business seeking to sort

out the way the management team works include ensuring that shareholder issues are separated from operational management issues. This is not just about ensuring the formalities are observed when running formal meetings of the shareholders (AGMs etc) with their panoply of Ordinary, Special and Extraordinary resolutions, and concomitant notice periods. It is common in the growing business for day-to-day operational issues to be lost in a discussion that is in effect about shareholder strategy. But issues of ownership are different from issues of management. Delegating to new professionals is exceptionally difficult for many founders used to getting their own way. And sticking to disciplined meeting structures can be even more difficult for a business used to the creative chaos which is characteristic of being

> **'In the first week of your new job** as FD of a growing business, you should try to avoid your accounts office. Spend the time on the "shop floor", talking to everybody and understanding the processes. Every evening, write down your thoughts for the day. At the end of the week, have a meeting with the MD and give him your initial impressions. Keep those notes you made. Look at them six months later. You will probably be amazed at how insightful you were in your first week, and also at how blinkered you have become in six months.'

small, where key decisions are taken over a sandwich, and 'strategy' is what happens down at the Dog and Duck. When the new finance director wanders past the CEO's office late on a Thursday night and sees the two founders arguing about something that was evidently too important for the agenda at that morning's newly instigated management meeting, it's easy for him to question the importance of his own contribution. Good practice is to ensure that the business is managed by management, via an operational board that meets regularly to consider reports on operational issues presented by managers responsible for the various areas.

> **'The FD needs to** "manage by walking around". In one hotel, the financial controller noticed that the bar takings increased significantly when the bar manager was on holidays. He questioned the bar manager, who attributed it to the weather. A chance comment from one of the bar staff uncovered the problem. It turned out that the bar manager had an extra till which he would bring into the bar at 6pm every evening. A good proportion of the night's takings would go into this till. At the end of the night, the till would be carried into the bar manager's car – and that revenue went straight into his pocket.'

Meetings typically might be fortnightly or monthly. Meeting attendees need not be company directors as recognised by Companies House – an individual's attendance is justified if she is responsible for an area of business activity. Agendas should include standing items to ensure all key operational areas are reviewed thoroughly. Separate meetings of the board itself should be convened on a regular basis (though less frequently than the operational team) to receive reports from the operational team and also to consider issues of broader import for the business, such as shareholder issues. This separation of responsibilities might all seem a bit too big-business for some, but the discipline is useful for even the smallest businesses as a way of ensuring that agendas are not confused and interests are not in conflict.

If the founder is serious about his new finance director, he has to be serious not just about changing meetings and management structure, but serious about changing the role he himself plays. 'I've seen entrepreneurs who embrace good people, and those who don't,' says one individual who has served as finance director with numerous growing businesses; 'the latter type of entrepreneur is foolish and needs help!' 'Good people' in this context include a good chairman – someone able to ensure meeting discipline, and able to ensure that operational management discussions are not confused with shareholder issues.

- A finance director has to understand what entrepreneurship is about
- A finance director and an entrepreneur have (and should have) different attitudes to risk. The finance director should make it his business to ensure each understands the other's attitude
- A finance director's first responsibility is to act in the interests of the company – not in the interests of the entrepreneur
- A finance director can establish credibility on the small things (expenses etc) as well as the big ones (corporate finance etc)
- A disciplined approach to management meetings should be implemented sooner rather than later

4

The finance director – and financial management

ONE ENTREPRENEUR KNOWS ALL about what he calls 'The unread information pack'. His biggest frustration is finance directors who are good at generating information. 'But I don't want information,' he says; 'I want knowledge.' On the other hand, a venture capitalist with considerable experience of dealing with entrepreneurs is not so confident that they know the difference. Many finance directors, according to

> **'The finance director's role** starts and finishes with business problems. In the middle there's a bit about cash and tax, but the business is where it starts and finishes.'

him, arrive to find that the team has been 'flying blind'. Companies fail, he worries, simply because of a cavalier approach to financial information. 'Never underestimate the ignorance of the entrepreneur,' notes one finance director. On the other hand many entrepreneurs find their finance directors too clever for them – whilst at the same time failing to understand the business itself. To do the job required, the finance director has to understand the business, its model and commercial drivers – as well as the technicalities of financial reporting.

The finance director and the entrepreneur have also got to understand each other.

Understanding the business is as much about capacity and attitude of mind as capability. If they're not careful, new

> **'In my experience** the FD of a growing business has to do a lot of basic accounting work, as she doesn't have the luxury of a team around her. In one situation, part of my FD role was very hands-on (more like a financial controller), involved in preparing accounts etc. I found that it was easy to get bogged down in that, and not to think strategically. The way I solved this was to have two different desks – one in the accounts department and one close to the MD's office. I would spend the morning in the accounts office and, at lunchtime, switch to my other desk, where I didn't have access to the accounting system on my computer. This forced me to switch into my "strategic" role for half of every day.'

finance directors find themselves falling into the role of financial controllers. But, as one property sector finance director observes, 'My role is 30 per cent finance and 70 per cent commerce.' Indeed, 'One of the first things I expect a good finance director to do is to hire himself a decent accountant as financial controller,' says one investor. 'This will help free up the finance director for the important stuff.' Commenting on the same issue, another finance director notes, 'The role of the financial controller is to keep the finance team out of the finance director's office.' Unfortunately, as noted earlier, finding and keeping a competent financial controller is perhaps even more difficult than finding a competent finance director.

In this context the relationship between the finance direc-

'The relationship between the finance director and the company's auditors and accountant is crucial.'

tor and the company's auditors and accountants is crucial. It isn't just big businesses such as Enron that get into trouble. There are situations when those involved in running small businesses need help, and in many instances accountants are well placed to assist. The problem that worries most entrepreneurs is not one of independence – it's one of efficiency and cost. Has an entrepreneur just spent a lot of money on me so that I can spend a lot of money on advisers? It is indeed critically important that the finance director keeps himself technically up to date. On the other hand a good adviser might well get to the right answer sooner. As usual with the growing business, there's a trade-off rather than a right answer.

Freeing up time for 'understanding the business' presumes an understanding of what is meant by 'understanding the business'. Finance directors in smaller businesses often find themselves having to 'get stuck in', with responsibility for wide areas of operational activity – often picking up human resources and facilities management, as well as the almost-impossible-to-avoid IT. But picking up the areas of management that the founder isn't interested in – no matter how

> **'Some FDs become obsessed** with the detail. One FD I worked for had a policy that you could claim a taxi when visiting parts of the operation only if it was raining. When she reviewed expense claim forms, she would phone the Met. Office to verify whether it had been raining in London at that time on that day.'

important they are – is not necessarily what 'understanding the business' is about. Nor does it have anything to do with an ability to step into the shoes of the entrepreneur himself. A wise entrepreneur doesn't look for an entrepreneurial finance director. As one seasoned finance director observes, 'Finance directors aren't even necessarily any good at business plans. They're too operationally focused. Not visionaries.'

In the words of one serial entrepreneur and business angel, 'The finance director has to show he understands the business (and is a businessman). He has to talk cash. And then he has to begin to establish numbers that show the key business drivers.' Of course, it is quite likely that the business founders themselves will not fully understand the drivers of success and the barriers to growth behind the business. A new finance director can add immediate value by passing his own personal analysis of the business to the founders whose success is a secret even to themselves. Such drivers and barriers are difficult to tease out, but are likely to remain hidden to someone interested in deploying financial levers alone. It might be something about the people, or the location, or the time in the economic cycle – as well as the product or service, the operation or the presentation. In an interesting bit of research on small and medium-sized enterprises, Dr Andy Neely and Dr Marek Szwejczewski of the Cranfield School of Management point to three non-financial levers as particularly influential on financial performance: overhead management, supplier management and people management.[11] A good finance director can influence management policy in all three of these areas – ensuring that overheads are kept in control; ensuring the business gets the best from its suppliers, and particularly that its leverage increases as the business grows; and ensuring that people management is disciplined and objective.

Information – and understanding it

Accounting information is just a way of telling a story. Some entrepreneurs want the story in as baroque or misleading a fashion as possible. As important as the story that is being told is the story that someone is trying to hide. Finance directors are more than just collators of information for supporting and analysing the present – they are storytellers and story interpreters. Often a genuine lack of financial understanding greets a growing business's first finance director. Professor Colin Barrow of Cranfield notes that when he ran his first programme there for owner-managers, by dinner on the first day it was obvious that 'twelve out of the twenty or so'

'Some things are exceptionally difficult to measure – particularly anything that has a human being at the heart of it.'

founders attending had a serious problem understanding the numbers. 'From seven o'clock that evening until one o'clock the following morning I ran an impromptu course on financial basics – understanding the P & L, that sort of thing.' Our own experience at BDO Stoy Hayward indicates that entrepreneurs can get quite a long way without really understanding some of the key financial dials. Part of growing up as a business, however, is being able – and willing – to read the dials that matter.

On the other hand too many accountants take too puritanical an approach to business control, citing that most malign of mantras: 'It's what gets measured that gets managed.' That the mantra is true for many is a condemnation of their business management methodology, and not a

> **'I joined an organisation** where there was a monthly management meeting. In my first week, I observed the meeting. Each department head produced a report outlining their main activities/achievements etc for the month, and what they were planning to do in the following month. At the next monthly meeting, as well as producing a management accounts pack, I also produced a similar monthly report. This was greeted with stunned silence. At the end of the meeting, the MD told me that there was no need for me to do this – he was only interested in the monthly accounts. He did not expect (or even want!) any output from the finance function except for the historical accounts and the occasional forecast.'

testimony to its successful application. Some things are exceptionally difficult to measure – particularly anything that has a human being at the heart of it. Numbers should not be relied on as ends in themselves when managing the business. Numbers are just one way in which the story can be told. The important issue is not whether you are able to *measure* but whether you can *tell the story* – and whether you understand it when it's told to you.

For example, systems and processes to generate information about the outside world are largely ignored in growing businesses. It comes as a surprise to many that small businesses often don't worry too much about the competition – they often see themselves as sufficiently differentiated to have discovered a competition-free niche for themselves, and sufficiently small to keep off the radar of big businesses who might see them as easy meat. Despite their obsession with selling, small businesses' information systems are often very inward looking. But systems are needed to keep an eye on what might be out there on the horizon. 'Gut feel' is not a substitute for looking at even the simplest piece of rational analysis of the market, customer demands, and competitor developments. The absence of reliable external information can become a problem very quickly as soon as your success catches the attention of big businesses who see your territory as a new opportunity when thinking about directions for expansion.

Though she needs to tread carefully, a new finance director in a growing business will have to influence the way the entrepreneur and other members of the management team 'read' the business, and their understanding of the key business levers and drivers. Most typical is the attitude of the entrepreneur to turnover, profit and cash. 'I worry about the top line and people issues only,' says one entrepreneur-client of ours. Conversely, in the words of one investor in small businesses, 'One of the key roles of the finance director is to wean the owner off turnover and on to margin.' Entrepreneurs are often salesmen first. Without a client or two all businesses are existing on borrowed time as well as borrowed money. But many entrepreneurs spend too long being too impressed by turnover. Turnover is vanity, profit is sanity – and cash flow is reality. As the finance director of a growing business you should be on the look-out for the temptation to succumb to pretty numbers – it is as easy to be vain with numbers as it is with words.

A good example of a failure to understand satisfactorily the balance between turnover and profit is often illustrated by attitudes to pricing. A price rise – even a small one – can have a dramatic effect on profit. A 10 per cent price increase will almost inevitably increase profit by a percentage much higher than 10 per cent. On the other hand a 10 per cent price cut might increase the volume of sales, but is likely also to reduce margin by much more than 10 per cent, with dramatic consequences. For example, with margins at 20 per cent, a business will need to increase sales volume by 100 per cent to maintain profit levels after a 10 per cent price cut. And even if such a strategy were successful in increasing absolute levels of profit, the *margin* might shrink to levels that threaten the balance of the cash cycle when the timing of cash flows are also taken into account. Many 'profitable' businesses have gone bust because they fail to generate enough cash at the right time to fund their growth.

The most critical time for pricing strategy is when new products are introduced. It is all too easy to under-price a new product. Increasing prices after a launch is much more difficult than increasing them before the launch.

Given that cash is so critical in young businesses it is not surprising that the first systems to appear are usually those

> **'You have to understand** the business and talk cash. Much of the rest you can leave to advisers.'

to control cash. Though often naive about profit, entrepreneurs are often careful about cash. Indeed, many entrepreneurs harbour the suspicion that clever accountants use numbers to tell whatever story they want, but fail to look after the stuff that matters. One of my favourite stories is that of the businessman who used to write cheques by hand for all his suppliers on receipt of invoice, but kept the cheques in the drawer of his desk in order of date due for payment. Every day he would review the cheques due for posting that day on an individual basis, taking a judgement on each before sending them out.

Though careful about cash, many entrepreneurs don't appreciate the amount needed to *grow* a business, and the relation of this both to the internal cash-generating capabilities of the business, and to external sources of finance. It is possible to determine mathematically from a business's cash generation the speed at which it can grow without seeking external capital.[12] But such an understanding is not really necessary for the entrepreneur – she just needs to understand the mechanics of working capital, appreciating the importance of getting the price for the product right, and knowing where, when and how the business breaks even.

Efficient credit control and supplier payment systems would be a good start for many young businesses. And efficient does not necessarily mean sophisticated. Financial dials in the growing business have to include mechanisms for looking at cash and profit. An analysis of debtor days and creditor days will give an entrepreneur information in the form of useful knowledge. If the creditor days are too long – to what extent are you concerned that you are risking your security of supply? If they are too short – to what extent are you not taking advantage of a potentially free source of credit? Monitoring the amount of value added per employee (gross profit divided by number of employees) – or even better, value added per employee pound (gross profit divided by staff costs) is an excellent way of plotting profit trends in a business that is changing rapidly. Measuring 'asset creep' (comparing categories of asset with turnover) can also help in an argument with other members of management about the vanity of turnover and the sanity of profit.

External financing

In addition to looking internally at a business's cash-generating capabilities and changing the dynamics of the cash cycle itself, the finance director will of course find himself in the front line when seeking external financing in the form of debt or equity investment. Again, it is dangerous to assume too much about the knowledge of the entrepreneur.

First there's the bank. UK businesses continue to rely on unstructured bank finance far too much for their own good (certainly when compared with businesses on the continent). Interest rates on overdrafts are on average 2.7 per cent above base, but can be as high as 8 per cent above (according to the Bank of England), and are notoriously unstable given that a bank can demand repayment whenever and for whatever reason it chooses. A longer-term loan is usually cheaper and more reliable. But debt-financiers will only lend if they can see a way of getting their money back. Bitter entrepreneurs bemoan the fact that bankers will give them money when they don't want it but will take away facilities when they need them most. But a loan that goes bad is a costly business for a bank that only makes money on a margin. It will not advance money unless it knows that its loan is secure, which offers some peace of mind to the bank, but is not going to be much comfort to the business.

Since the last recession, banks have been more careful and sensible in their lending, and their claims of being more sensitive to the particular needs of smaller and growing businesses are by and large true. Certainly there has been an increase in the popularity of forms of loan finance that more flexibly match the growth of the business. Asset-based lending is on the increase. Debtor factoring and/or invoice discounting was once thought of as the corporate equivalent of a visit to the pawnshop, but no longer. Though relatively expensive, forms of finance such as this at least have the merit of growing with your working capital requirements: as your debtors grow, the amount you can borrow grows too. They can also help mitigate the problem of debt-collection.

But a finance director taking up a new position in a growing business may find the business funded by friends and an overdraft. Putting financing on to a more stable footing will depend a lot on the relationship between the business – the finance director in particular – and the bank manager. Indeed, one investor in growing businesses told us that when recruiting he is always on the lookout for 'the finance director whose wife and bank manager don't understand him'. The relationship is more complex – and should be more complex – than is often thought, or can be gleaned from bank adverts. 'I expect the FD to stand up to the bank where necessary,' says one venture capitalist. 'The problems of banks start with their literature,' comments another observer. 'They're there to convert one asset into another more liquid asset. They're not there to help you.' Perhaps more pragmatically a finance director notes, 'Bankers are there to be negotiated with. Too many assume even in small businesses that you're just supposed to say yes or no.'

The *nature* of the relationship with the banker is of great importance. 'It's important *not* to have a personal relationship with your bank manager,' argues one entrepreneur. 'Banks should play a minimal role in business development.' Even where disclosure is concerned the entrepreneurial

'The relationship between the FD and the bank manager is more complex than is often thought.'

viewpoint might be described as robust. 'Always be straight with the bankers,' argues one entrepreneur known to us. 'Well, *almost* always,' he quickly adds; 'I suppose I'm not so much interested in honesty as I am in credibility.'

Finance directors, perhaps understandably, tend to be a bit less distant. 'Investors and lenders tend to expect obfuscation from the owner,' says one investor. 'But then they'll turn to listen to the finance director.' One finance director reckons he calls his bankers every month. 'After September 11, 2001 I was calling them every week,' he comments. 'There's a real danger when the bank manager changes and the new guy doesn't understand the business – or you find the old one has been allowing the business too much slack,' observes an investor. And as an investor he expects even the finance director to be a little cautious in his disclosures: the finance director 'does and should play straight man to the entrepreneur,' he says. 'But although the finance director should tell the financier everything he wants and expects to hear, I still expect him to have another ten per cent up his sleeve ...'

Few companies funded solely by debt grow fast. Part of the role of the finance director is to help the owner to under-

> **'A good finance director** can help an entrepreneur understand when equity is equity, and not debt masquerading as equity.'

stand the role and value of equity finance – and also to distinguish between true equity finance and debt finance. 'Beware labels: many venture capitalists don't really invest in equity – they invest in debt,' argues one observer. 'They share all the rewards and none of the risk.' Is this bitterness or is it pragmatism? 'Business angels tend to be more honest ... they don't have the structures for fostering the clever manoeuvring of figures.'

The act of giving away equity can be a painful experience for an entrepreneur. Giving away equity may appear expensive – entrepreneurs are acutely aware that in the long term equity finance involves giving away part of the value of your business. But it may be the difference between a business that survives and one that doesn't. Giving away equity doesn't involve giving away control of the business unless you give away more than 50 per cent, or unless a Shareholder Agreement gives veto rights to a minority. Nevertheless, history is full of entrepreneurs who have confused absolute ownership with control, and whose reluctance to consider equity funding until too late has resulted in the death of the company.

Financial controls

In addition to financial information and financial management a finance director taking up a new role in a growing business will often have to pay close attention to internal financial controls. The internal control environment is likely to be weak. In the early days the founder probably signed everything and regarded this as an effective form of financial control. There is unlikely to be any form of internal audit. An entrepreneur is likely to interpret 'segregation of duties' as the right to his own office rather than a key component of a financial control environment. But as the business has grown management attention will have been stretched. And the entrepreneur will have to understand that having a capable finance director involves more than just having another 'honest' member of the senior team with signing powers. Unsurprisingly, research indicates that SME finance directors consider fraud less of a problem than do big company finance directors by a factor of 2:1. This reflects complacency rather than a lack of sophistication or concern, born out of a belief

'A new finance director has an important role in setting the right tone for a good control environment, ensuring that good apples don't turn into bad ones.'

that the people you know are more honest than those you don't, and the assumption that fiddles are perpetrated by crooks rather than ordinary human beings under pressure and presented with an opportunity. An entrepreneur who has put friends and family in positions of power is often compounding the problem.

A new finance director has an important role in setting the right tone for a good control environment, ensuring that good apples don't turn into bad ones. Unlike the big listed business, fraud in a small business is less likely to occur in and around the production of financial statements (other than at the time of business transfer). In the early days the finance director may well make sure that attention is paid to seemingly small things (petty cash, expense accounts), but he should also see to it that 'financial control' extends to recruitment processes and the establishment of an effective 'whistleblowing line'. He will ensure that attention is paid to informal sources of information as well as the formal business dials; you should always listen to gossip as there may be some truth there. He should also fight for the time and money required to set up the environment before a crisis exposes the need for one. Companies don't like spending money on preventative work, not least as it's impossible to measure the benefits immediately, but it's a battle worth fighting. At the same time the finance director needs to make sure that the control environment isn't propped up by a framework that is too constraining and inflexible. Flexibility will demand frequent adjustment. After all, it is not small companies that beat large companies, but fast and agile companies that beat slow and inflexible companies.

- Many successful entrepreneurs haven't a clue about finance and have been successful despite it
- The finance director's focus should be on cash and profit rather than the turnover many business founders are obsessed with. Turnover is vanity, profit is sanity, and cash is reality
- Growth hides weaknesses in systems, control, strategy etc, which a finance director has to identify
- The finance director has to understand the business before he can direct the finance
- Management is about much more than measuring and managing what can be measured
- The relationship between the business and its bankers is key and the finance director should make it his responsibility

5

Where the buck stops

FAILURE IS AN IMPORTANT REALITY when running small and growing businesses. Running a growing business and having run a failed business are equally valid facets of entrepreneurship. Finance directors who hope to be involved in such businesses will obviously work hard to avoid economic Armageddon – but they are no more immune from it than the entrepreneurs themselves. In the US entrepreneurs wear their business failures as badges of pride. Some will cite them on their CVs. In the UK business leaders are a bit more coy.

Nevertheless, a finance director in business with an entrepreneur should know exactly where his own and his company's fortunes stand in the event of business turning bad. Given that business failure is such an ever-present threat it is startling how little directors know about the key regulations governing the area and the extent of their own responsibilities and liabilities. The potential costs of failure are significant and the career damage can be long term.

A finance director in an entrepreneuerial business has to know with absolute clarity if and when the end may be near. Key tests for insolvency are when the company is unable to pay its debts as they fall due, or it can be proven to the satisfaction of a court that the value of its assets is less than its liabilities (including contingent and prospective liabilities).

'A finance director in an entrepreneurial business has to know with absolute clarity if and when the end may be near.'

Knowing when the end is near is of course dependent on the state of an organisation's financial information systems. If your early warning systems flash early enough it may be possible to avoid Armageddon, or to ride out what may be just a bad patch. In a young business, warning systems in and around cash flow and margin should be particularly sensitive – and directors should worry about negative trends as soon as they manifest themselves. It should be remembered that the human capacity for turning a blind eye to negative indicators is startling. The benefit of hindsight is often an excuse for failing to believe what was in front of your eyes at the time. A decline in value added per employee pound is a particularly good early warning indicator that the business model is not in quite the shape it needs to be. But perhaps most important

of all is an absolutely pragmatic approach to cash management – knowing who can be stretched and how far when cash is short. Getting priorities right is critical. And don't expect government agencies to be too happy with being put low down the list. One of the 'FAQs' on the Customs and Excise website seems to offer hope to the afflicted. 'I am not able to pay the debt immediately because of a temporary "cash flow" problem. What should I do?' is the question. 'Make urgent contact with your bank or your financial adviser to explore means of overcoming these temporary financial difficulties,' is the less than helpful answer C&E give to their own question.

Understanding definitions of insolvency is critical in particular so that directors can avoid the perils of 'wrongful trading' – trading when the directors know or ought to know that the company is unlikely to avoid insolvent liquidation.

'Wrongful trading' can have serious implications including personal liability for the director, and a very real risk of being disqualified. When a business gets into this much trouble a director needs to appreciate an important shift in his allegiance: from owing duty to his shareholders, he starts to

---

The order of payment of creditors in a formal insolvency is often forgotten:

1 Secured creditors holding fixed charges (up to the value of their security)
2 Preferential creditors (including government agencies – though this is likely to change soon – and unpaid employees up to certain levels)
3 Creditors holding floating charges
4 General creditors
5 Shareholders

---

have a duty to his company's creditors. A director must be proactive to avoid personal liability in these circumstances – ensuring he is aware of the approach of insolvency, and is doing something about it. A director of a business close to reaching the definition of insolvency should take advice from a licensed insolvency practitioner.

It is not just wrongful trading that can bring disqualification. Any insolvency brings the risk of disqualification for the director if he is considered to have been inept or careless in the running of the company. Indeed, an insolvency practitioner supervising a formal insolvency has to report to the DTI on anyone who was a director at any time within the three years prior to the commencement of the insolvency. The onus therefore is absolutely on the directors to ensure they act responsibly. Directors of companies treading close to the line should be very careful, for example, not to give preferential treatment to any creditors. It should not be forgotten that there are degrees of disaster, and acting responsibly sooner rather than later can be much the safest option. Creditors' Voluntary Arrangements might sound drastic – but companies have survived them and gone on to prosper. A Compulsory Winding Up order, like death, is something altogether more final. Furthermore, finance directors bearing bruises and scars from the recession in the early 1990s should note a significant difference of attitude as the economy teeters on another brink. Financiers are much more sympathetic to the importance of turnaround and regime now. Even government regulation is changing to reinforce this change of attitude. But you can't help a business unless it tries to help itself. If you're in trouble, get help fast.

Notes about corporate death cannot possibly be complete without paying serious attention to the personal exposure of directors. In the post-Enron, post-Worldcom world the responsibilities and duties of directors are being taken more seriously than before. In a big business there will probably be advisers inside and outside the business spending time and a relatively small percentage of company profit trying to ensure that directors and their companies stay the right side of regulation. (Whether they choose to take any notice, of course, is another matter.) In the smaller, growing business the buck will often start and stop with the directors.

There is perhaps no better way to highlight the extent of directors' responsibilities than by working your way through a list of the most worrying ways in which directors might find themselves called personally to account – and pay – for the misfortunes of their companies. For the nervous a list is included at the back of this book. It is surprising how few directors appreciate the sensitivity of their personal positions to their own professional mistakes. A finance director would be unwise to seek comfort in the fact that he is not a lawyer and therefore not expected to have a high level of knowledge. But in the land of the blind the one-eyed man is king – and the FD should work hard to make sure that he meets few surprises, and that everyone else on the board is spared surprises

> **'Many growing businesses** appoint friends into non-executive director roles. Often, these people have never been a non-exec before. I try to take them aside very early on, and explain the rules and issues about directors' responsibilities, insolvent trading etc. This tends to scare them and they become much more interested in the cash flow after that.'

as well. Keeping up to date technically is obviously critical. Also important is meeting and sharing ideas with other finance directors. The one-eyed man is lonely as well as king in the land of the blind, and should seize every opportunity to network and join peer groups.

So much for the concept of the limited liability company, you might think. But it's worth remembering that limited liability was designed to protect the shareholders, not the directors. In performing her role the finance director has to ensure that she is at one with the board, but also apart from them. A good finance director should get on with the rest of the board, but should not be their puppet. She is the eyes and ears of the board, but in many ways has to think for them rather than with them. She also has to master the art of not being liked when this is necessary. And she may have to face up to the likes of the stockbroker who was asked for help at a time of crisis, as an unfortunate entrepreneur remembers: 'You ask for help. Well, I will do one thing for you – I will come and feed the buns to you through the bars at Brixton Prison.'

- ▥ Failing is part of succeeding
- ▥ Look out for failure, prepare for it and know what you will do when it happens
- ▥ Understand the definitions of insolvency – and their consequences for the future of your business and your own career
- ▥ Watch out for the natural tendency to disbelieve indicators you don't want to believe
- ▥ Learn from your mistakes!
- ▥ Understand when the personal liabilities of the directors may be put to the test
- ▥ The finance director in a small business is usually the one the board will rely on to see them safe
- ▥ If in doubt take advice – particularly if the business is dicing with insolvency

6

And in the end

AS IMPORTANT AS THE BEGINNING is the experience at the other end – as the business comes out of the entrepreneurial phase.

How you define this rite of passage is a matter of opinion. For some it's a question of size – numbers of employees, financial performance. For others it's more a question of ownership. It might mean either a listing on the Alternative Investment Market or a full Stock Exchange listing. Given that the experience of being a finance director in the growing business is tied up so much with the evolution of the founding team, for many the key rite is the 'exit', for whatever reasons and by whatever means, of the founders.

A business soon to lose its founder is a business soon to be without the personality that has got it this far. Organisational culture fills the gap vacated by the personality of the founder. Culture is just one abstract construct that needs to be managed. In these later stages, the concept of brand also begins to become important. Culture ties the organisation together internally, and brand is the way in which that culture manifests itself to the outside world. As Simon Gulliford (brand management guru) has observed, businesses do not have a choice as to whether or not they have a brand, but they do have a choice as to whether or not they manage their brand. Managing this sort of thing is a very different experience from that provided by the trials and tribulations of early growth companies.

A business with a life independent from its founders and its managers has a corporate image that needs developing and maintaining both internally and externally. The business has a complexity and multiplicity that reflects the fact that an increasing number of stakeholders have an interest in it and expect to be heard by its directors. The business has responsibilities as employer, property owner, consumer, investment vehicle, political fulcrum and producer. Indeed, it is more than likely that the business conceives of itself as a network of businesses rather than as one – perhaps with different parts of the empire at different stages of evolution. Again this means a fundamental change in the nature of the role of the directors: even if they founded it, their business is no longer theirs.

A full listing or trade sale is likely to be the most significant financial transaction to confront any growing business. If you go this far you will be taking counsel from texts a lot fatter and more comprehensive than this one – in fact from professionals in their offices rather than from books at all. It is critically important that directors, no matter how accomplished or experienced, take advice from professionals. And well-advised directors might well take advice on their advice. Make sure your advisers are experienced for your situation – and are not using you as a case study.

When you're going through this sort of transaction, by and large you should expect to pay lots for good advice. Take the contracts that govern the transaction, for example. The lawyers drafting the contracts may know a lot about con-

'The business has a complexity and multiplicity that reflects an increasing number of stakeholders.'

tracts, but even good lawyers may not really understand the full implications of some of the accounting terminology which the contracts purport to define. It is important that directors, lawyers, accountants and bankers are fully aware of the detail behind the deal, have been there before and know exactly what they are doing.

Taking advice from lawyers, accountants and bankers may sound like professional costs cubed – and it is indeed expensive. But it is a lot less expensive than clearing up the mess afterwards.

Of course, the founder-owner is likely to find the experience harder even than other members of the team. No role changes more than that of the founder as the business evolves, and it is a rare individual who can steer a business successfully through all the stages of evolution from start-up to large, sustainable business. The fact that the few who do get a lot of national press coverage should not fool anyone into thinking that such individuals are anything more than the exceptions that prove the rule. Indeed, many founders have stayed on too long and damaged their businesses and their fortunes. The rule is that the founder will and should seek an exit, and it is a question of when, not whether. This can come as quite a surprise to the entrepreneur – particularly remembering that entrepreneurship is often a reaction against something. As one of my clients put it: 'Endgame? We're just happy to be in a game – we haven't really thought about the endgame!' With a founder 'looking for an out', however, even more pressure will be foisted on to the senior members of the team who remain – with the job not just of helping to groom the business, but also of helping to maintain leadership and control as the founder's attention begins to wander.

Relationships with financial stakeholders are more complicated and are likely to be the source of considerable tension. For many who are ambitious for growth, the move to a stock market listing and away from owner-managed status is a rite of passage. But running a business under the scrutiny of institutional investors is a very different experience from running it under your own scrutiny. Richard Branson bought Virgin back from the shareholders in 1998 saying, 'Being an entrepreneur and the chairman of a public company just don't mix.' Andrew Lloyd Webber in similar circumstances described flotation as 'an absolutely enormous, crashing mistake'.[13] 'Did flotation work?' Anita Roddick of The Body Shop asked herself in a lecture to promote her book, *Business as Unusual*, in Edinburgh in August 2001. 'Yes, it did,' she said, but continued, 'It gave us money to build manufacturing plants. Does it work now? I don't think so.' The Body Shop had 'lost its soul' since floating on the stock market, and had no place as a 'cog in the international finance system'. 'The Body Shop is now really a dysfunctional coffin.' She noted that there had been two attempts to take the company private, where it could avoid the harsh light of investor scrutiny and the pressure of market forces. In a surprise move in April 2002, Stelios Haji-Ioannou resigned as chairman of EasyJet at the age of 35. 'Starting a company requires a very different skill-set from those needed to chair a major PLC, and I consider my strengths are in the former,' he said. 'The history of the City is littered with entrepreneurs who held on to their creations for too long, failing to recognise the changing needs of the company.'[14]

Is this an argument against taking the entrepreneurial business public? No, I don't think so – but it is evidence that some directors are not fully aware of the consequences or the costs of taking their businesses through this final growth hurdle. Again it is the finance director who should be best placed to prepare the team. Whether she chooses to stay around afterwards to take on the role of finance director to the listed business, with the public scrutiny, conference calls with analysts, and pressure to deliver from institutional investors that this involves, is ultimately a personal choice.

Getting this far is a measure of success. But it might be a sign that it is time to start all over again.

- ▓ Directing a grown business is a fundamentally different experience from directing a growing business
- ▓ Founders leave. It's not whether, it's when

7

Useful information

Size triggers

It's not just the businesses themselves that change as they get bigger – it's also the rules that govern them. Here is a selection of key size triggers.

Some employee trigger points

- If you have fewer than 5 employees you are exempt from the requirement to prepare and distribute a written statement of health and safety policy etc.
- An employee who is not given her job back, nor offered a suitable alternative job, at the end of her *additional* maternity leave will not be automatically regarded as unfairly dismissed if the employer employs five or fewer people immediately before the end of the additional maternity leave period and it is not reasonably practicable for her to be taken back in her original job or offered a suitable alternative. NB: this exemption applies to additional maternity leave only, and not ordinary maternity leave.
- When you have 5 or more employees, you have to offer a stakeholder pension scheme (unless you already offer an

occupational pension scheme that all staff can join within a year of joining the firm, or offer employees access to a personal pension scheme that meets certain conditions, in particular one about the employer contributing an amount equal to at least 3 per cent of each member's basic salary).

- If you have fewer than 15 employees you are exempt from the Disability Discrimination Act, which says that it is unlawful for an employer to discriminate against a person on the grounds of their disability in the recruitment process or in the workplace. But NB: from 2004 the Disability Discrimination Act is likely to cover all employers, regardless of size.
- If you have fewer than 20 employees you are exempt from the requirement to give details of your disciplinary scheme and grievance procedures in your Statement of Terms of Employment. This exemption is likely to be removed from 2003.
- When intending to make 20 or more employees redundant at one establishment within a 90-day period, employers have a legal obligation to consult employee representatives, as well as to consult employees individually. (NB, if you make fewer than 20 employees redundant, you still have an obligation to consult them individually.)

Financial triggers

'Small' companies are exempt from audits if their:

- Turnover is £1 million or less
- Assets are £1.4 million or less

'If you have fewer than 5 employees you are exempt from the requirement to prepare a written statement of health and safety policy.'

Companies may file small company abbreviated accounts if they have two of the following:

- Turnover of £2.8 million or less
- Balance sheet total (i.e. total assets) of £1.4 million or less
- 50 employees or fewer

Companies may file medium-sized company abbreviated accounts if they have two of the following:

- Turnover of £11.2 million or less

- Balance sheet total of £5.6 million or less
- 250 employees or fewer

You must register for VAT if your taxable turnover is expected to exceed £55,000 (2002 figures) in the next 30 days. (If not, you can choose to register for VAT anyway.)

Businesses with turnover of less than £125,000 and taxable turnover of less than £100,000 can register for the 'flat-rate' VAT scheme, allowing them to calculate VAT owed by applying a flat-rate percentage to turnover. (Watch out! – this *may* have the effect of costing you more.)

Businesses with turnover of less than £600,000 can use the VAT cash accounting scheme, where VAT returns are based on payments made and money received in a period rather than with reference to invoice dates.

Key deadlines for private companies

Tax

You must register with the Inland Revenue within 3 months of setting up in business (including when becoming self-employed).

Payment dates

PAYE	19th of each month
Class 1A NIC payment	19 July (after tax year)
Corporation tax	9 months and 1 day after the end of the accounting period (unless making more than £1.5 million taxable profit, in which case tax is payable in instalments)

Income tax	First payment, 31 January (in tax year)
	Second payment, 31 July (after tax year)
	Balance, 31 January (after tax year)

Tax returns and forms

Corporation tax	12 months after end of accounting period
Personal tax	31 January (after tax year)
PAYE annual return	19 May (after tax year)
P14	19 May (after tax year)
P60s to employee	31 May (after tax year)
P11D & P9D	6 July (after tax year)

(see www.inlandrevenue.gov.uk)

Notifying Companies House

Accounts filing	10 months after the year end
Annual return	Within 28 days of the date on the form
Change of directors' details	Within 14 days of change
Special, Extraordinary and some Ordinary resolutions	
	Within 15 days of resolution
Mortgage and charges	Within 21 days
Allotment of shares	Within 1 month of allotment

(see www.companieshouse.gov.uk)

Directors' liability

Ways in which directors might incur personal liability include:

- When a director gives a personal guarantee, e.g. to the company's bank or landlord. It's hardly helpful to advise a director to avoid personal guarantees wherever possible, when in many situations banks won't lend without them. But, at the risk of stating the obvious, they are a lot easier to sign than they are to get rid of. And, as with many commercial arrangements, directors often forget that you might be able to negotiate on terms – e.g. expiry dates and triggers. Indeed, failing to pay attention to the small print can spring nasty surprises. One business leader I know once opened his door to an official instigating proceedings as a consequence of a personal guarantee given in connection with a lease on a property he had vacated years ago when working for another business with which he had long since ceased to be associated.

- Directors can be personally liable on contracts made by them on the company's behalf when the director has not made it clear that he is contracting as an agent of the company, and the name of the company is not correctly set out on invoices, cheques etc.

- In the event of non-compliance with prescribed information and disclosure requirements relating to the contents of a company prospectus inviting the public to subscribe for the purchase of any shares or debentures in the company. This can be as onerous as it sounds. Indeed, if a prospectus contains false or misleading statements, both civil and criminal proceedings may be initiated against both the company and the directors who authorised its issue. Directors should also watch out for being personally sued for negligence or deceit in the case of misrepresentation. Genuine ignorance or honest mistakes provide defences in some circumstances.

■ If the company commits an offence a director might find herself considered as having committed a parallel statutory offence if she authorised or consented to the offence, or merely (knowingly) allowed it to be committed. The Health and Safety, and Environment regulations are especially worth looking out for.

■ If a director knowingly allows his company to continue trading when he knows or ought to know that there was no reasonable prospect of avoiding insolvency (i.e. wrongful trading), a court may order the director to pay any loss suffered by any creditor.

■ Fraudulent trading is a step worse than wrongful trading, and may result in a fine or even imprisonment. It is cold comfort to note that fraudulent trading is something that can catch anyone – not just directors.

■ If he manages a company whilst disqualified from acting as a director, an individual will be personally liable for the debts of that company.

■ If she fails to comply with the requirement to obtain shareholders' consent for the personal purchase or sale of an asset from/to the company, the director may well be personally obliged to make good any loss suffered by the company or even the profits made in the process.

■ If a company pays a dividend unlawfully (e.g. without having sufficient distributable reserves) the directors may be held liable.

■ Failure to provide obligatory Employers' Liability Insurance could result in an employee seeking to recover damages from the directors.

■ Employment of illegal immigrants is a criminal offence and may result in action against the directors as well as the company – particularly if the former have connived at the offence or have been negligent.

■ Knowledge of offences committed under trade description legislation could give rise to personal liability for a director – as well as two years in prison.

■ Persistent failure to make returns to the Registrar of Companies may result in disqualification from being able to act as a company director.

Other reading

There's notoriously little out there worth reading on the small business and the growing business. But if you are interested in finding out more the following might be useful and are all easily available via the usual book sources.

■ M. Baghai, S. Coley and D. White, *The Alchemy of Growth*, Orion Business, 1999

■ A. Bhide, *The Origin and Evolution of New Businesses*, OUP, 2000

■ S. Birley and D. Muzyka, *Mastering Enterprise*, FT Pitman, 1997

■ E. Flamholtz and Y. Randle, *Growing Pains*, Jossey-Bass, 2000

■ P. Leach, *The BDO Stoy Hayward Guide to the Family Business*, Kogan Page, 1991

■ G. Moore, *Crossing the Chasm*, Capstone, 1991

For technical information about deadlines, regulations etc, the government's web pages get better all the time. Start with www.dti.gov.uk or www.inlandrevenue.co.uk and go from there.

8

Acknowledgements

BOOKS, no matter how short, are always collaborative efforts. This one has benefited from discussions and draft readings from several of my partners at BDO Stoy Hayward, including in particular Simon Bevan, Mike Haan, Andrew Durant and Peter Leach.

More particularly the book has benefited from the insights and anecdotes of our clients and professional contacts – including in particular the following who gave significantly of their time and wisdom: Colin Barrow, Jon Gooding, Barry Green, Maurice Marks, Jitesh Patel, David Williams, and Charles Boundy of Fladgate Fielder. I'd like to make special mention of Stella Donoghue – a wonderful source of anecdote and experience.

Lastly I thank Joanna Merson, for forbearance when I was paying her no attention at all during the late nights I was drafting and redrafting the manuscript, and also for reminding me of the usefulness of tax deadlines etc. But then she was born on 6 April …

In business writing as in all forms of enquiry there is very little that is original. I've tried to give credit where credit is due. I apologise if I haven't. Of course, if I've misunderstood someone else's ideas, deliberately or otherwise, the fault is all mine.

9

Notes

1 Quoted in S. E. Finer's *The History of Government*, Vol. I (OUP, 1997)

2 Abraham Zaleznik seems one of the earliest – *Harvard Business Review*, May 1977

3 John Kotter uses this diagram to contrast leadership and management in *Leading Change* (HBS, 1996)

4 'Leadership and Management', J. S. Newman, *Business Growth and Profitability*, January 1997

5 'The Questions Every Entrepreneur Must Answer', *Harvard Business Review*, November 1996, but see also Bhide's great book *The Origin and Evolution of New Businesses* (OUP, 2000)

6 'Let them eat sushi': Simon Rogers, *RSA Journal*, Vol. CXLV, No. 5476, January 1997

7 M. Beer & N. Nohria: 'Cracking the Code of Change', *Harvard Business Review*, May–June, 2000

8 e.g. *The Woman Entrepreneur*, R. Hisrich and C. Brush (Lexington Books, 1985)

9 For an interesting discussion of this in the context of negotiation see 'Why Negotiations Fail: An explanation of barriers to the resolution of Conflict', R. Mnookin, *NIDR Forum*, 1993

10 Speech to the RSA, November 1996, reported in *RSA Journal*, Vol. CXLV, No. 5476, Jan/Feb 1997

11 'Performance of SMEs: an analysis of the benchmark index', A. Neely and M. Szwejczewski, Cranfield School of Management, quoted in *The Growing Business Handbook*, 4th edition (Kogan Page, 2001)

12 An excellent presentation of this thinking is to be found in J. Mullins and N. Churchill's article – 'Cash Cows or Cash Hogs? Three Levers for Managing Cash in Growing Companies', *Harvard Business Review*, May 2001

13 Quoted in *The Times*, coincidentally on April Fool's Day, 1995
14 Quoted in the *Financial Times*, 19 April 2002

Current and forthcoming BDO titles

Non-executive Directors
A BDO Stoy Hayward Guide for Growing Businesses
by Rupert Merson

The role of the non-executive director has never before come under such scrutiny. From once being seen as 'about as useful as Christmas tree decorations', non-executives are now seen as critical components in the corporate governance framework, and important contributors to the strategic health of companies.

Rupert Merson explores the particular contribution the non-executive can make in the younger, growing, owner-managed business.

ISBN 1 86197 499 X

£6.99

Managing Directors
A BDO Stoy Hayward Guide for Growing Businesses
by Rupert Merson

Part inventor, part entrepreneur, part manager, part accountant, part leader, part salesman, part bottle-washer – the role of managing director in the younger, growing business is one of the most demanding jobs in commerce today. Yet it is surprisingly little written about. Rupert Merson plugs the gap with another of his insightful, irreverent, but as always informative guides.

ISBN 1 86197 682 8

£6.99

An Inspector Returns
The A–Z to surviving a tax investigation
by Daniel Dover & Tim Hindle
with cartoons by Michael Heath

Revised and updated second edition

If you are the subject of a tax investigation by the Inland Revenue, do not panic – read this book instead. An investigation undoubtedly means trouble, but the straightforward advice in these pages should help steer you around the worst pitfalls and survive the process intact.

'An amusing guide through this difficult subject … This disarmingly honest little book could save you many sleepless nights.' *The Times*

ISBN 1 86197 420 5

£6.99

War or Peace
Skirmishes with the Revenue
by Daniel Dover & Tim Hindle
with cartoons by McLachlan

Each year over 250,000 people are subject to Inland Revenue enquiries. It is not a pleasant experience. But help is at hand. For the first time here is a book that explains the whole process, along with numerous tips on how to proceed and what to do – or not to do. Deftly written with wit and humour, this could save you time, misery and money.

ISBN 1 86197 524 4

£6.99